GHOSTS
IN SOUTH AMERICA

BY NICOLE E. RODRIGUEZ MATA

EPIC

BELLWETHER MEDIA • MINNEAPOLIS, MN

EPIC BOOKS are no ordinary books. They burst with intense action, high-speed heroics, and shadows of the unknown. Are you ready for an Epic adventure?

This edition first published in 2022 by Bellwether Media, Inc.

No part of this publication may be reproduced in whole or in part without written permission of the publisher. For information regarding permission, write to Bellwether Media, Inc., Attention: Permissions Department, 6012 Blue Circle Drive, Minnetonka, MN 55343.

Library of Congress Cataloging-in-Publication Data

Names: Rodriguez Mata, Nicole E., author.
Title: Ghosts in South America / Nicole E. Rodriguez Mata.
Description: Minneapolis : Bellwether Media, 2021. | Series: Global ghost stories | Includes bibliographical references and index. | Audience: Ages 7-12 | Audience: Grades 4-6 | Summary: "Engaging images accompany information about ghost stories in South America. The combination of high-interest subject matter and light text is intended for students in grades 2 through 7"-- Provided by publisher.
Identifiers: LCCN 2021011324 (print) | LCCN 2021011325 (ebook) | ISBN 9781644875414 (library binding) | ISBN 9781648344497 (ebook)
Subjects: LCSH: Ghosts--South America--Juvenile literature. | Haunted houses--South America--Juvenile literature.
Classification: LCC BF1472.S63 R64 2021 (print) | LCC BF1472.S63 (ebook) | DDC 133.1/298--dc23
LC record available at https://lccn.loc.gov/2021011324
LC ebook record available at https://lccn.loc.gov/2021011325

Editor: Betsy Rathburn   Designer: Brittany McIntosh

Printed in the United States of America, North Mankato, MN.

TABLE OF CONTENTS

GHOSTS
IN SOUTH AMERICA

South America is a continent known for its dark jungles. Mountains and deserts also cover the land.

The landscape is the setting for many strange stories. Could South America be filled with ghosts?

EL SILBON

Venezuela

El Silbón is a Venezuelan ghost.
He wanders through the plains at night.

6

El Silbón carries a bag of human bones with him. He is searching for more to add to his collection!

THE WHISTLER

El Silbón is Spanish for "the whistler!"

El Silbon looks like a tall, skinny man. He whistles a creepy tune. When he is far away, his whistle is very loud. His whistle is quiet when he is near. Run away!

El Silbón is only afraid of three things. Barking dogs scare him away. Whips and spicy peppers do, too.

But the best way to avoid him is to stay inside at night!

LA LUZ MALA

Strange balls of light float through the South American countryside at night. They are mostly found in Chile, Argentina, and Uruguay.

Uruguay

Chile

Argentina

12

A CREEPY NAME

La Luz Mala means "the bad light" in Spanish!

The lights are called La Luz Mala. They are often red or white. Stories say they are restless souls seeking justice.

Most of the time, the lights stay far away. But sometimes, they chase people! The only way to escape is to run away and pray. What could the lights be?

CULTURAL CONNECTION

The Australian Outback is home to strange lights. They float near the ground at night. They are known as the Min Min Lights.

A HAUNTED HOUSE

La Casa Matusita is a creepy house in Lima, Peru. In the 1700s, a strange woman moved in.

She had no friends or family. People thought she was a witch. They sentenced her to die.

Lima
Peru

Stories say the woman cast a spell on the house. Anyone who entered would be cursed!

Since then, visitors have seen terrifying sights. They have heard laughter and screams.

IS IT TRUE?

There was once a government building near La Casa Matusita. Some believe the curse was made up to keep people away from it!

La Casa Matusita

Eventually, the house got a new owner. It was remodeled. Some old parts were taken away.

Many think the curse is now broken.
Others believe it still lingers.
What do you think?

GLOSSARY

continent—one of the seven main land areas on Earth

cursed—put under a harmful spell

justice—fair treatment

lingers—remains

plains—large areas of flat land

remodeled—fixed or improved

sentenced—gave a punishment by a court of law

TO LEARN MORE

AT THE LIBRARY

Alexrod-Contrada, Joan. *Haunted Houses Around the World*. North Mankato, Minn.: Capstone Press, 2017.

Klepeis, Alicia Z. *Peru*. Minneapolis, Minn.: Bellwether Media, 2019.

Koontz, Robin. *Great Minds and Finds in South America*. Vero Beach, Fla.: Rourke Educational Media, 2020.

ON THE WEB

FACTSURFER

Factsurfer.com gives you a safe, fun way to find more information.

1. Go to www.factsurfer.com.

2. Enter "ghosts in South America" into the search box and click ᗧ.

3. Select your book cover to see a list of related content.

INDEX

The images in this book are reproduced through the courtesy of: SL-Photography, front cover (top), p. 5; Oomka, front cover (bottom), pp. 2-3; Ruslana Iurchenko, p. 3; Fred Chaveton, pp. 4-5; EmilioAl26, pp. 6-7; Lucy.Brown, p. 7; elcatso, p. 8; Michal Szymanski, pp. 8-9; Cyrsiam, p. 9; Volodymyr Burdiak, p. 10; klemen cerkovnik/ Alamy, pp. 10-11; Carlos Mauer, pp. 12-13; Ko G.capture, p. 14; AlexVH, pp. 14-15; Zsolt Czillinger, pp. 16-17, 19 (bottom); Fotos593, p. 17; Vladimir Mulder, p. 18; Africa Studio, p. 19 (top); Peruvian Art, pp. 20-21; Ironika, p. 21; dani3315, p. 22.